A Maze Me

POEMS FOR GIRLS

A Maze Me

POEMS FOR GIRLS

By

Naomi
Shihab Nye

PICTURES BY

Terre
Maher

Greenwillow Books
An Imprint of HarperCollins Publishers

I am grateful to the Lannan Foundation and the town of Marfa, Texas.
—N.S.N.

A Maze Me: Poems for Girls

"Every Cat Has a Story" appeared in *Instructor.*

"Little Blanco River" appeared in *Poetry from A to Z,* edited by Paul Janeczko.

"Messages from Everywhere" appeared in *Creative Classroom.*

"Mona's Taco" appeared in *The Texas Observer.*

The text of this book is set in 12-point Garamond 3.

Book design by Paul Zakris.

Library of Congress Cataloging-in-Publication Data

Nye, Naomi Shihab.

A maze me : poems for girls / by Naomi Shihab Nye ; illustrated by Terre Maher.

  p. cm.

"Greenwillow Books."

ISBN 0-06-058189-1 (trade). ISBN 0-06-058190-5 (lib. bdg.)

1. Girls—Juvenile poetry. 2. Children's poetry, American. 3. Maturation (Psychology)—Juvenile poetry. [1. Girls—Poetry. 2. Self-actualization (Psychology)—Poetry. 3. American poetry.] I. Title: Amaze me.
II. Maher, Terre, ill. III. Title.

PS3564.Y44S94 2005 811'.54—dc22 2004003283

First Edition 10 9 8 7 6 5 4 3 2 1

 Greenwillow Books

In memory,
Precious Nina
Precious Rubina

And for Jamie and Lyra Iris Skye,
Jenny and Lyda Rose,
Daria and Josephine

Contents ～～～～～～～～～～～～～

SECTION THREE ∽ Magical Geography

SECTION FOUR ∾ Sweet Dreams Please

SECTION FIVE ∾ Something True

Introduction

At twelve, I worried about a skinny road between two precipices. Every day my mother drove on such a road, or so I imagined, to her job teaching school. I feared her car would slide off one side, into a ditch, or off the other edge, into a murky gray river. But I never told her what I was scared of. I worried day after day without mentioning my fear to anyone, till there was a fist in my stomach, punching me back again and again to check the clock. Wasn't she late? I was a nervous wreck in secret.

I did not want to be thirteen, which cast me as something of an oddity among my friends, who were practicing with lipstick and the ratting hair comb deep into the belly of the night. Mary couldn't wait to be thirteen. She stuffed her bra, packed away her dolls. Susie had been pretending she was thirteen for two years already. Kelly said thirteen was a lot more fun than anything that preceded it.

But I did not feel finished with childhood. I was hanging on like a desperado, traveling my own skinny road. The world of adults seemed grim to me. Chores and complicated relationships, checkbooks that needed balancing, oppressive daily schedules, and the worrisome car that always needed to have its oil or its tires changed ("bald tires" sounded so ominous) . . . Couldn't I stay where I was a bit longer?

I stared at tiny children with envy and a sense of loss. They still had cozy, comfortable days ahead of them. I was plummeting into the dark void of adulthood against my will. I stared into the faces of all fretful, workaholic parents, thinking condescendingly, *You have traveled too far from the source. Can't you remember what it felt like to be fresh, waking up to the world, discovering new surprises every day? Adulthood is cluttered and pathetic. I will never forget.*

I scribbled details in small notebooks—crumbs to help me find my way back, like Gretel in the darkening forest. Squirrels, silly friends, snoozing cats, violins, blue bicycles with wire baskets, pint boxes of blackberries, and random thoughts I had while weaving 199 multicolored potholders on a little red loom. I sold the potholders door to door for twenty-five cents each, stomping around the neighborhood, feeling absolutely and stubbornly as if I owned it. No one else had ever loved that neighborhood as much as I did.

If I wrote things down, I had a better chance of saving them.

Recently, a friend sent me an exquisite wreath in the mail. A tag was attached to it: A SMALL AMOUNT OF

DEBRIS IS TO BE EXPECTED FROM THE VIBRATION OF
SHIPPING.

Well, of course.

But who tells us this when we are twelve? Who
mentions that the passage from one era into another can
make us feel as if we are being shaken up, as if our contents are shifting and sifting into new alignments?

Earliest childhood: skillets and a fat soup pot and two
cake pans and a funny double boiler with lots of little
holes in one pan, lids and a muffin tin and two blue
enamel spoons and an aluminum sifter with a small
wooden knob on its handle, all living together in the
low cupboard next to the stove.

A trove of wonders! Daily I was amazed and happy
to take them out, stack them on the floor, bang them
together a little, make a loud noise. Then I could put
them back. There were ways they fit and ways they
didn't. The door to the cabinet never shut perfectly. I
can close my eyes even today and feel its crooked wood,
its metal latch, and the lovely mystery of the imple-
ments living in silence inside.

My mother worked at the sink nearby, peeling pota-
toes, running water over their smooth, naked bodies. I
felt safe. My whole job was looking around.

~~~~~~

It strikes me as odd: I cannot remember the name of a single junior high school teacher. I cannot remember any of their faces either. Yet I recall all my elementary and most of my high school teachers very clearly. What happened in between?

In junior high, I stood proudly in the percussion section in the school band, smooth wooden drumsticks in my hands. I clearly recall the snappy beats we played to warm up. I still feel my cheeks flaming when I was forced to sit down, runner-up in the spelling bee, because they gave me a *military* word. I remember the smooth shiny hair on the back of the head of the girl in front of me in Spanish class better than the subjunctive tense in Spanish. Some things stayed, during those rough years of transition, but not the things I might have dreamed.

What do you want to be? people always ask. They don't ask *who* or *how* do you want to be?

I might have said, *amazed forever.* I wanted to be curious, interested, interesting, hopeful—and a little bit odd was okay too. I did *not* know if I wanted to run a bakery, be a postal worker, play a violin or the timpani drum in an orchestra. That part was unknown.

Thankfully, after turning seventeen I started feeling as if my soul fit my age again, or my body had grown to fit my brain. But things felt a little rugged in between.

In college I met Nelle Lucas, who wore billowing

bright cotton skirts and lavish turquoise-and-silver Native American jewelry. She taught ceramics (favoring hand-building techniques—coiling, rolling, smoothing) and showed us how to prepare our own basic hand-mixed glazes. I think I took her class three times.

Nelle and her husband had built some modest, rounded Navajo-style hogans out in the Texas hills, and on weekends, they shepherded little flocks of art students to the country. We dug a big hole in the ground to fire our pots and sang songs while the pots baked under the earth. Sometimes the pots disappointed us—blowing up, or cracking. One person's pot might compromise someone else's—after exploding, fragments stuck to your own precious glaze. Or someone's glaze would drip strange configurations onto your perfect iron oxide surface. It was a tricky operation. Nelle sneaked wisdoms into every line of art instruction. She wasn't terribly impressed with anyone's pots, but she loved the process and she loved us all. Also, she made us laugh. She *experimented*. We slept in a circle, head to toe. We patted whole-wheat chapatis, cooking them over an open fire for our breakfast. Nelle loved freshly mixed granola, wild deer, and patience. She urged us to slow down and to pay better attention to *everything.* She was radiant, enthusiastic, unpredictable. And she was older than all our parents.

Somehow, knowing Nelle when I was in college gave me all the faith about "growing up" I needed. At every age, a person could still be whimsical, eccentric. A person could do and think whatever she wanted. She could be as spontaneous at seventy as at seven. I felt incredibly relieved.

Midway between Brady and Mason, Texas—two wonderful hill-country towns—there's a mysterious general store called Camp Air. A small red stagecoach sits out front, and a little sign says the store is closed on Fridays and Saturdays, but I have never seen it open. Some cows with very short legs are penned up nearby, next to a "watermelon shed." There's a larger sign: HEY IF YOU NEVER STOP YOU'LL NEVER KNOW WHAT YOU MISSED. I always stop. And I still don't know. But I like it. I like it a lot. "Camp Air" has a good ring to it. That's where I want to live, every day, inside my timeless brain.

If you have a voice, and aren't afraid to spend it . . .

If you have many voices and let them speak to one another in a friendly fashion . . .

If you're not too proud to talk to yourself out loud . . .

If you will ask the questions pressing against your forehead from the inside . . .

you'll be okay.

If you write three lines down in a notebook every day (they don't have to be great or important, they don't have to relate to one another, you don't have to show them to anyone) . . .

you will find out what you notice. Uncanny connections will be made visible to you. That's what I started learning when I was twelve, and I never stopped learning it.

Every year unfolds like a petal inside all the years that preceded it. You will feel your thinking springing up and layering inside your huge mind a little differently. Your thinking will befriend you. Words will befriend you. You will be given more than you could ever dream.

—NAOMI SHIHAB NYE
San Antonio, Texas, 2004

SECTION ONE

Big Head

Rose ~~~~~~~~~~~~~~~~~~~~~~~~

A very large spider
wove her fancy web
between the Don Juan rosebush
and the Queen's Crown vine.
We greeted her every day
going in and out.
We had so many destinations
but she just swung there
in the air
in the day's long stare
that grows so hot by four o'clock
we boycott the whole front yard.
By evening we'd be outside again
breathing jasmine
watering honeysuckle
plucking mint
and she'd be wrapping
her little flies and wasps
in sticky sacks.
The trolley rang its bell at us

and we waved back.
It was nice living with Rose.
Living our different lives
side by side.
One night wild thunder
shook the trees,
the sky crackled and split,
the winds blew hard
and by morning
Rose was gone.
Did she wash away?
Did she find a safer home?
She keeps spinning her elegant web
inside us
so long
so long
after the light made it shine.

Mystery

When I was two
I said to my mother
I don't like you, but I like you.

She laughed a long time.

I will spend the rest of my life
trying to figure this out.

Ringing ~~~~~~~~~~~~~~~~~~~~~~~~~

A baby, I stood in my crib to hear
the dingy-ding of a vegetable truck approaching.

When I was bigger, my mom took me out
   to the street
to meet the man who rang the bell and
   he tossed me
a tangerine . . . the first thing I ever caught.
   I thought he was
a magic man.

My mom said there used to be milk trucks too.
   She said, *Look hard, he'll be gone soon.*
And she was right. He disappeared.

Now, when I hear an ice-cream truck chiming
    its bells, I fly.
Even if I'm not hungry—just to watch it pass.

Mailmen with their chime of dogs barking
up and down the street are magic too.

They are all bringers.
I want to be a bringer.

I want to drive a truck full of eggplants
down the smallest street.
I want to be someone making music
with my coming.

Toys on the Planet Earth

We need carved wooden cows, kites,
small dolls with flexible limbs.
I vote for the sponge in the shape of a sandwich.
Keep your bad news, world.
Dream of something better.

A triangle mobile spinning in the wind.
Furry monkeys hugging.

When my dad was small,
his only toy was an acorn and a stick.
That's what he told me.
So he carved the acorn into a spinning top
and wrote in the dirt.
And that's what made him
the man he is today.

Every Cat Has a Story

"British researchers found that a sheep can distinguish and recognize as many as 50 other sheep's faces for up to two years, even in silhouette." (NEWSPAPER REPORT)

The yellow cat from the bakery
smelled like a cream puff.
She followed us home.
We buried our faces
in her sweet fur.
One cat hid her head
when I practiced violin.
But she came out for piano.
At night she played sonatas on my quilt.
One cat built a nest in my socks.
One inhabited the windowsill
staring mournfully up the street all day
while I was at school.
One cat pressed the radio dial,
heard a voice come out, and smiled.

Visiting My Old Kindergarten Teacher, Last Day of School

She's packed the brown bear puppet
in the cupboard and distributed
the Self-Portraits with Hats.
I remember those.
She says, "You look just the same
but bigger! I would know you anywhere!"
I would know her too.
Someone's crying.
He doesn't like the little holes
in the corner of his painting
from hanging on display.

I help her gather stubs of crayons
from the table grooves.
Do the plans she made on the first day
seem far away
as pebbles dropped into a stream?

The ones whose names she calls in her sleep
gather rumpled papers into their bags,
hug her and fly.
It is a big wind blowing
after they all go home.

Worry ~~~~~~~~~~~~~~~~~~~~~~~~~~~~~~~~

My mother's braid
is wrapped in soft tissue
and stored in a shoebox
in the attic.

I don't want to be
eighty years old
looking at that braid
all by myself.

The Boys

I played with the boys till I felt blurry.
Minicars, fast cars,
the model ship constructed with toothpicks and glue.

WHOOOOOOOOO-EEEEEEEEEEEEEEEEEEEE!
(*that* was boring)

The boys went running into the field waving sticks!

The boys hit a fire hydrant with a stick and laughed!

Where Are You?

When I was small,
I called out through the house.

I'm here, said my mother and dad.
I'm here, said my brother,
and the bear on my bed
said it too.

In your bones
in your memory
      trust me

I'm tucked inside each fresh paper page
you'll write on.
Each hour you don't see me, I'm still there.
How many things add up the same?
Your life, my life,
      the bucket, the sea.

Ellipse ~~~~~~~~~~~~~~~~~~~~~~~~~~~~~~~~

My father has a parenthesis
on either side of his mouth.
His new words
live inside his old words.
And there's a strange semicolon
birthmark on my neck—
what does it mean,
my sentence is incomplete?

Please,
live with me in the open slope
of a question mark.
Don't answer it!
Curl up in a comma
that says more, and more, and more . . .

Big Head, Big Face

(what my brother said to me)

If your head had been smaller
maybe you woulda had less thoughts in it,
maybe you wouldn't have so many troubles.
This is just a guess but seems to me
like a little drawer only hold a few spoons
and you can always find the one you need
while a big drawer jammed with tongs
strings corks junky stuff receipts birthday cards
you never gonna look at
scrambled and mixed so one day
  you
open that drawer
poke your hand in and big knife go
  through your palm
you didn't even know a knife was IN there,
well, that's why I think
it might not be so bad to have a little head
with just a few thoughts few memories few hopes
maybe if only one little one came true
that be enough for you.

Supple Cord ~~~~~~~~~~~~~~~~~~~

My brother, in his small white bed,
held one end.
I tugged the other
to signal I was still awake.
We could have spoken,
could have sung
to one another,
we were in the same room
for five years,
but the soft cord
with its little frayed ends
connected us
in the dark,
gave comfort
even if we had been bickering
all day.
When he fell asleep first
and his end of the cord
dropped to the floor,

I missed him terribly,
though I could hear his even breath
and we had such long and separate lives
ahead.

Every Day 〰〰〰〰〰〰〰〰〰〰

My hundred-year-old next-door neighbor told me:
every day is a good day *if you have it.*
I had to think about that a minute.
She said, Every day is a present
someone left at your birthday place at the table.
Trust me! It may not feel like that
but it's true. When you're my age
you'll know. Twelve is a treasure.
And it's up to you
to unwrap the package gently,
lift out the gleaming hours
wrapped in tissue,
don't miss the bottom of the box.

The Bucket

A small girl with braids
is carrying a bucket
toward the sea.
She walks determinedly,
her red bathing suit
secure on her hips.
She seems to know
exactly what she is doing,
what she will carry
in the bucket.
Nothing can stop her,
not the sand,
which tries to swallow
each tiny foot,
or the mother,
calling after her
with a camera.
Now she is running,
waving her arms,
the small bucket
thrown free
into the air!

Little Chair ~~~~~~~~~~~~~~~~~~

"There's a cool web of language winds us in. . . ."
—ROBERT GRAVES
"I saw great things mirrored in littleness. . . ."
—EDITH SITWELL

1

I didn't mind so much
growing out of little girl clothes
the blue striped shirt
the corduroy jumper
giving up Candy Land
and my doctor's kit
but never again to fit
the turquoise Mexican chair
with flowers painted on it
hurt

I keep it in my room till now
a throne for the stuffed camel
Little kids sit on it when they visit
The straw in the seat is still strong
The flowers are always blooming

2

Miss Ruth Livingston
who taught first grade for forty-three years
in Marfa, Texas
kept a little reading chair
in front of the windows in her classroom
Whenever her students finished their work
they knew they could go over to the little chair
and read
It was a safe place
Their minds could wander anywhere
I wish everyone in the world had a little chair

3

Recently a big cowboy wearing sunglasses
came to Miss Livingston's house and asked where
"that old furniture from our classroom went"
She's ninety-seven now
She still has her china-faced dolls
from when she was small
She pointed at the wooden reading chair
sitting in front of the windows
in her beautiful living room
He walked over to the little chair
with his hands folded
and silently stood there, stood there

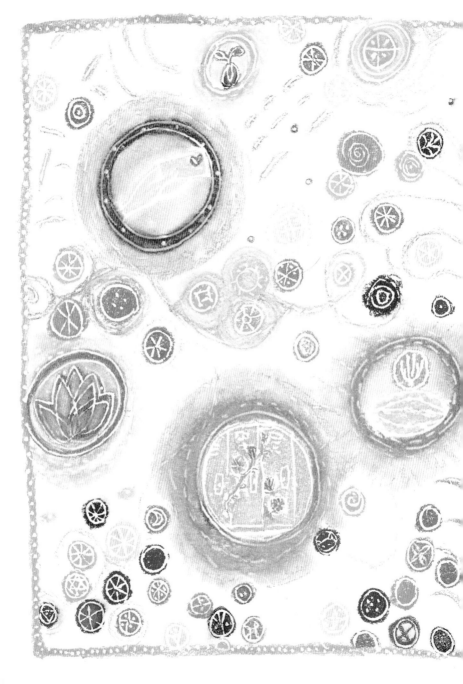

SECTION TWO

Secret Hum

Secret

How can I be in love with a bus
going by at 6 A.M.
when no one I know is riding it?

Swoosh of tires in the rain—
the hummingbird in the zinnia patch
doesn't find a single flower worth
sinking her beak into.
She's a choosy hummingbird!

            I'm a choosy hummingbird

All day I dip and dive

twice as alive

as yesterday.

Some Days ~~~~~~~~~~~~~~~~

Your handwriting stands
like a small forest on the page
You could enter it anywhere

Your room looks new to you
maybe you moved a lamp
arranged a pillow differently
on the bed

Such small things
change a room

Single candle
on a desk you finally cleaned
sharpened pencils waiting
in a white cup

I devote myself to short sentences
Air answers
Breath remembers
A streak of light signs the floor

Eye

I am keeping my eye on that boy.
My secret eye, spy eye.
How does he act when the teacher
leaves the room?
If someone makes a mistake,
what then?
He picked up Lucy's pencil when she dropped it.
Does he recognize my existence?
Does he see me gleaming
in my chair?

I Want to Meet the Girl

who does not run her country
the way I do not run my country.

I want to meet the girl
who hides in a crowd,
who laughs into her hand,
who was not in the picture.

The girl who stands back
after being introduced
by her parents
in a way she would not choose.

Who turns her head to the side
so she doesn't miss seeing what's there.
Where is she?

In the School Cafeteria

Your face makes me feel like a lighthouse
beaming across waves.
We don't even know one another,
yet each day I am looking for your face.
Walking slowly among tables, I balance my tray,
glancing to the side.
You're not here today.
Are you sick?
Why are you absent?
And why, among all these faces,
is there only one I want to see?
Whatever the reason
your absence is not excused
by me.

Crush

A girl wrote a letter on an orange
and placed it on a doorstep.

That day the sky tasted fresh as mint.

Where He Is ~~~~~~~~~~~~~~~~~~

Last night at sunset
two jet trails made a giant X in the sky
right over our city.
I was reading Spanish in the porch swing
when my neighbor walking her two dogs
pointed up, shouting happily,
 "X marks the spot! YOU ARE HERE!"
White trails against dusky blue.
I stared at her. I said, "You are here too.
We are all here."

And I got goose bumps.

Because I knew the boy I haven't met yet
is here too, somewhere close by,
and I knew he was looking up.
I could feel him looking.

Groups of People
Going Places Together ~~~~~~

One is always walking
           in front of the others.
Maybe this is the one
who really wanted to come.
They didn't all want to come,
           that's for sure.
Someone is pushing a baby carriage.
The baby is sleeping, sunburned,
           or fussy.
           Maybe the baby didn't want to come.
           The baby would rather be
                   crawling around on a rug.

That girl would rather be home reading.
Very little conversation
      is going on.
Maybe two people tipping their heads together
asking why they came.
No one smiles at me or anyone else going by.
      They are clumsy, carrying towels, jugs,
          beach bags, hats.
It is hard to walk in a group.

Sifter ∿∿∿∿∿∿∿∿∿∿∿∿∿∿∿∿∿∿

When our English teacher gave
our first writing invitation of the year,
Become a kitchen implement
in 2 descriptive paragraphs, I did not think
butcher knife or frying pan,
I thought immediately
of soft flour showering through the little holes
of the sifter and the sifter's pleasing circular
swishing sound, and wrote it down.
Rhoda became a teaspoon,
Roberto a funnel,
Jim a muffin tin
and Forrest a soup pot.
We read our paragraphs out loud.
Abby was a blender. Everyone laughed
and acted giddy but the more we thought about it,
we were all everything in the whole kitchen,
drawers and drainers,

singing teapot and grapefruit spoon
with serrated edges, we were all the
empty cup, the tray.
This, said our teacher, *is the beauty of metaphor.*
It opens doors.
What I could not know then
was how being a sifter
would help me all year long.
When bad days came
I would close my eyes and feel them passing
through the tiny holes.
When good days came
I would try to contain them gently
the way flour remains
in the sifter until you turn the handle.
Time, time. I was a sweet sifter in time
and no one ever knew.

I Said to Dana's Mother

I can't wait to be older and free.
We were sitting at Dana's kitchen table,
working on our history project.
Free of schoolwork, able to choose
the ways I spend my days,
but Dana's mom turned her face
to me sharply.
"Missy," she said (not my name),
"you'll never be as free
as you are now."
Then she turned back to
cooking dinner.
The air felt thinner in the room.
Thinner, and sad.
Can air feel sad?

Because of Poems

Words have secret parties.
Verbs, adjectives, and nouns
meet outside their usual boundaries,
wearing hats.

MOODY feels doubtful about attending
and pauses near the door, ready to escape.
But she's fascinated by DAZZLE.
BEFRIEND throws a comforting arm
around her shoulder.

LOST and REMEMBER huddle
in the same corner, trading
phone numbers.

I serve punch.

Having Forgotten to Bring a Book, She Reads the Car Manual Aloud

Do not sit on the edge of the open moonroof.
Do not operate the moonroof if falling snow
has caused it to freeze shut.
(I thought it was a sunroof, actually.)
Do not place coins into the accessory socket.

The cup holder should not be used while driving.
Well, when then?
While parked at home?
Perhaps at midnight, with insomnia?
Hi, Mom, I think I'll just go have a glass of milk
in the driveway.

If you need to dispose of the air bag
or scrap the vehicle . . .
Never allow anyone to ride in the luggage area.
Do not operate the defogger longer than necessary.
Please remove necktie or scarf while working on
engine.
Never jack up the vehicle more than necessary.

A running engine can be dangerous.

If the Shoe Doesn't Fit

you take it off
of course you take it off
it doesn't worry you
it isn't your shoe

On the Same Day
My Parents Were Arguing

Down by the quiet little river
between the old missions,
white cranes stand listening.

It is hard to tell if they are awake.

Their elegant necks barely turn
as another crane floats low
among them, touching ground.

One dips a beak swiftly into water
then springs back.

What have they seen across the long sky?
It hides inside the layered feathers
of their heads.

Changed ~~~~~~~~~~~~~~~~~~~~~~~~~~~~

They said something mean about me
and didn't notice it was mean.

So my heart wandered
into the rainy night without them
and found a canopy
to hide under.

My eyes started
seeing through things.
Like gauze.
Old self through new self.
My flexible body
went backwards
and forwards
in time.

It's hard to describe but true:
I grew another head
with better ideas
inside my old head.

Hairdo

Because of the hair on the head
of the girl in front of me in school,
daily I travel slopes and curves.
I detour past the ribbon.
The clip is a dam.
I want to pluck it out—
surprise!

Inventing new methods for parting
on a blue-lined page, I make
math go away.
Embrace the math of hair.
Layers and levels of hair.
Some hair grows into ropes.
Rivers of waves, blunt cut.
Oh what will I make of my messy messy hair?

Message in the Thin Wind
Before Bedtime ~~~~~~~~~~~~~

Stiff lip won't help.
Stiff arm breaks too.
You need soft touch.
Try on soft shoe.

Hard voice cracks back.
Hard head heats up.
Mark that sharp note.
Bypass "So what?"

Tender heart lasts long.
Who looked? Who heard?
Let those grips go.
Birds get last word.

High Hopes ～～～～～～～～～～～～～～～

It wasn't that they were so
high, exactly,
they were more
low-down,
close-to-the-ground,
I could rub them
the way you touch a cat
that rubs against your ankles
even if he isn't yours.

So yes I feel lonely without them.
Now that I know the truth,
that I only dreamed someone liked me,
the cat has curled up in a bed of leaves
against the house and I still have to do
everything I had to do before
without a secret hum
inside.

Bad Dream ~~~~~~~~~~~~~~~~

None of the cats
will let me touch them

I bring clean bowls
of fresh milk

They won't drink it
till I'm back in the house

Tuxedo cat looks up
I'm at the window

Flick! He ran
into the bushes

Is this what it feels like
to grow older and return to

the neighborhood
you once knew?

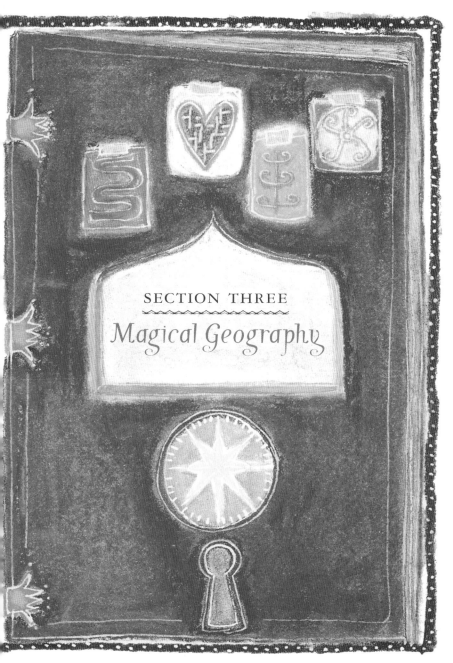

SECTION THREE

Magical Geography

People I Admire

poke their shovels into the dirt.
Whatever they turn over interests them,
not just what they plant.
If there are roots or worms,
if the soil is darker, or mottled,
maybe the cap of an old bottle,
a snail, an ancient tunnel
left by a burrowing mole.

They know there is plenty of ground.
Every place has a warm old name.
The plumed grasses bend backwards
in the breeze, their job in life,
and they are proud of it.

My Body Is a Mystery

My body is a mystery
      a magical geography of skin
It keeps me in

      And I travel in it everywhere
sometimes it seems to beat me there
and then we meet again

Oh my eyes are the windows
      and my face is the sky
And my legs are the trees that hold me
My hands are the branches and my head is a box
      and I spend my lifetime picking locks

My body is a symphony
      a tuba and a piccolo and drum
           I hear some drum

And it sometimes seems to beat so low
And other times it makes me want to run
              and then I have to run

Oh my blood is the music
        and my voice finds the notes
And my lungs are conductors singing *One! Two!*
        And I sometimes lose the melody but I
never lose the dream
        of the songs that might come through

Because my body is a mystery
           a magical geography of skin
that keeps me in
          And I travel in it everywhere
        sometimes it seems to beat me there and then
We meet again
            Oh we always meet again

Feeling Wise ～～～～～～～～～～～～～

A lady was quoted in the newspaper.
"It is not so hard to feel wise.
Just think of something dumb you could say,
then don't say it."

I like her.
I would take her gingerbread
if I knew where her house was.

Julia Child the famous chef said,
"I never feel lonely in the kitchen.
Food is very friendly.
Just looking at a potato, I like
to pat it."

Staring down
makes you feel tall.
Staring into someone else's eyes
makes you feel not alone.
Staring out the window during school,
you become the future,
smooth and large.

Sometimes I Pretend

I'm not me,
I only work for me.

This feels like
a secret motor
chirring inside my pocket.

I think, *She will be so glad*
when she sees the homework
neatly written.

She will be relieved
someone sharpened pencils,
folded clothes.

Poor Monday ~~~~~~~~~~~~

At the stoplight
faces in the next window
are plaster-cast ceramics,
blank, unoriginal.

At school my friends drag in glumly.
Our teacher says, "What can you expect?
It's Monday."

So what?!
I'm Naomi!
You're Rosa Lee!

Watermelon Truck

Today a truck heaped with watermelons
at the corner—
   fat, stacked bodies
      striped like animals

The sign said "75 cents and up"
An old man shaded his head with a newspaper

"And up"—the great American twist
You know he meant one midget for 75

   The other hundred, $3.50

Margaret

May I describe the contents
of my grandmother's kitchen
in Nova Scotia in 1949?
Grinding mill, butter churn,
hand-hemmed white cotton towels,
pale purple swatch of linen
spread diagonally
across a scarred wooden table
where Grandmother
kneaded and stirred.
A platter rimmed with violets,
some of the petals rubbed away.
And the crock of wooden spoons, of course,
the giant matches in a box . . .
There was something in the oven, always,
a streak of patience in the air.

My Sad Aunt

She sits in the living room,
mad at my parents
because they won't let her
smoke in the house.

Maybe it's not always easy
having a good imagination.

It follows you around
till you're not sure who that is,
sitting in the living room.

She remembers a dream
that didn't come true.

A riverbed
with no water in it.

Who did she want to be
when she was younger?

The List ~~~~~~~~~~~~~~~~~~~~~~~

A man told me he had calculated
the exact number of books
he would be able to read before he died
by figuring the average number
of books he read per month
and his probable earth span,
(averaging how long
his dad and grandpa had lived,
adding on a few years since he
exercised more than they did).
Then he made a list of necessary books,
nonfiction mostly, history, philosophy,
fiction and poetry from different time periods
so there wouldn't be large gaps in his mind.
He had given up frivolous reading entirely.
There are only so many days.

Oh I felt sad to hear such an organized plan.
What about the books that aren't written yet,
the books his friends might recommend
that aren't on the list,

the yummy magazine that might fall
into his view at a silly moment after all?
What about the mystery search
through delectable library shelves?
I felt the heartbeat of forgotten precious books
calling for his hand.

You're Welcome!

Where has courtesy gone?
(MY GRANDMOTHER'S CHANT)

People who don't say "Thank you"
are a mysterious tribe.
Who do they think
they are?

People who say "No problem"
instead of "You're welcome"
have a problem they don't even
know about.

Moving House

A whole house traveled
down Broadway yesterday.
An old-fashioned white house
with green trim . . .
traffic stopped
so the house on wheels could pass.

You could almost hear
the lost family laughing,
clink of dishes,
swish of a screen door
in summer heat.

I wanted to follow the house,
to see where its new landing place would be,
but we were on a shopping trip
(faucets, tile, sinks)
for our very stationary house
that hasn't gone anywhere
in a hundred years.

Actually, my mom and I were tired,
wishing we didn't have to shop.
Seeing the moving house
changed us.
Everything felt easy after that.

Making a Mosaic

Some people begin at the center,
others at the outer edge,
pressing down chips
of lovely broken plates and cups.
Is this the story of days?
Arranged, glued down,
without much space between.

Here is the blue flowery fragment
from dinnerware
on a ship
that sank in 1780.
The antique green plate
Louise gave me
when I finished fifth grade.
Side by side,
a nice time, a terrible time.

It's a messy job,
glue stuck to fingertips.
You keep standing back
to see a pattern
emerge.

Necklace

I hope Sunday's slow and long,
steeped like a pot of mint tea.
Soft sun and deep thinking.

Saturday was a crowded calendar page,
a mound of chores.

Could Monday be a porch?
Facing the week.
Wednesday a meadow?

Thursday, let's leave
small baskets at everyone's door.
Flowers, notes, stones.
No one does that anymore.

Could a week be strung on a silver chain?
A boat?
A tree?
Tuesday as a tree?

From Labrador, 1800s ~~~~~~~

*"If you wish to know who I am, I am old Lydia Campbell,
formerly Brooks, then Blake, after Blake now Campbell. So,
you see, ups and downs has been my life all through. And
now I am what I am . . . "* (A CANADIAN ORAL HISTORY)

We are who we are.
Lydia, we send you light
from far away.
We send you green from a warm place.
You who knew the ice and cold,
who grew old inside your many names,
what were you like
before it all happened?
What did you hope
and where would you have
wandered?
Did you ride on a sled pulled by dogs?

When you stared into the swirl
of green northern lights in a midnight sky,
did you think those icy fingers
were pointing at you,
did you whisper, "Hi there,"
feeling the little hairs
on your skin
stand straight up?

SECTION FOUR

Sweet Dreams Please

Historical Marker ~~~~~~~~~~~

out here in the land of wind
little purple flowers
where people once fought

it's hard to imagine
people finding one another
in this huge space

and having something to fight about

Baby-sitting Should Not Be Called

sitting. Because it is chasing, bending,
picking up, and major play.
It is helping Wiley throw eight basketballs
into a green wheelbarrow and getting them out
again and doing this one hundred
times. Then he sits on the second step
to roll basketballs off the edge.
He waves at me to give them back.
Then he pitches pecans
at the tree trunk and wants me
to retrieve them.
They are small and
hide in the leaves.
But he knows if I find the right one.
Also he wants me to climb the ladder
(only to the third step)
holding him under one arm
so he can poke the fat basketball
through the lowered hoop.
Sitting? That's a joke.

He wraps the baby doll
in a piece of green tissue paper
and eats Cheerios at the same time.
No! He doesn't want me to
give the baby doll a Cheerio!
He wants to roll cars into
a parking lot in the corner
and speed them over my feet.

Wiley helps me remember
where I came from. I love him for
more than one reason.
I love his clean purpose,
his careful eye.
His pure glee when the pecan hits hard
and bounces off.
I love baby-sitting
even though I have to sleep
stretched out flat
like the monkey without stuffing
afterwards.

Abandoned Homestead,
Big Bend National Park ~~~~~~~~~

Gilberto Luna and his wife
raised nine children
in this stone house
off the gravel canyon road.
They grew corn and peppers
between the dry lips of the desert.

Did his children ever fight?
What did they dream of,
so far from any city or train?
I think they dreamed of a fossil
full of clouds.

Gilberto lived to be extremely old.
Deserts will do that.
What about his wife?
The walls tipped in soon after they died.
Houses miss their people too.
A hundred years later, thin slits of light
sneak into three crooked rooms.

Turtle

Tonight I read a newspaper story
about a turtle found in Virginia
key on a key chain
looped through a hole in his shell
a number engraved on the key
the man who found him called the number
far away in Pennsylvania
learned that turtle was let loose twenty years before
Ho!
Think about it:
all these years of our lives,
        he's been walking.

Little Blanco River ~~~~~~~~~~

You're only a foot deep
under green water
your smooth shale skull
is slick & cool
blue dragonfly
skims you
like a stone
  skipping
    skipping
it never goes under
you square-dance with boulders
make a clean swishing sound
centuries of skirts
lifting & falling in delicate rounds
no one makes a state park out of you
you're not deep enough
little blanco river
don't ever get too big

The Bird Pose ~~~~~~~~~~~~~~~~

For two months I examined
the photo in my mom's yoga book.
It looked so easy,
balancing your knees
on your elbows.
But mine kept collapsing
like portable chairs.
My mom said, *Remember, you
have to start slow.*
How slow is slow? I said.
This feels slow to me.
Nothing helped so I threw the book
back on my mom's bed.
What a dumb thing I tried to do.
That night I dreamed I flew.

Meteor Watch ～～～～～～～～

Leaving the car on a high hill in the dark,
we spread a tablecloth on the ground
and eat with our fingers—
grapes, gingersnaps, cheese—
staring at the huge sky.
This night feels ripe.
What will flash by?

We want stars to surprise us.
We want to be
amazed.

Each streak of light, we cry out.
If you turn your head
for just a minute, you can miss one.
Focus on east,
you lose the ones in the west.

I think of people knowing one another
in the great spaces,
the brave arc of connection
between friends, lit up.
And all the quiet stars
holding their places in between.

Writing in a Silo

I used to translate what a hen said.
Little kids believed me.
I looked deep into a cat's eyes
to speak her language.

Memory is a silo
—what's stocked
up?—

Corn or sorrow?
Crumbs of wheat
speckled hope?

1 door
2 windows
is this
a blossom
or a day?

What would I dream if I slept in a silo?

Standing by the train track
I wrote something different
than I might write
in a library.

When I sat by the river
my words became brown ducks
dipping their heads.

Finding a Pink Ribbon on the Wilderness Trail

We went hiking on the edge of town,
saw three deer, an armadillo
with coarse hairs on his belly when
my dad turned him over.
He snorted like a little pig.
Golden eagles flew huge circles
around their nests.

Then I found a lost ribbon on the trail,
the kind I would be sad to lose,
satiny smooth, with no rips
or blemishes.
I picked it up and put it in my pocket.
Later I worried.
What if the girl who lost it came back
looking for it?
We are tied by a trail,
tied by a ribbon.
I hope someone nice
finds the things I lose.

Bird in Hand ∿∿∿∿∿∿∿∿∿∿∿∿∿∿

She was trying to show
the baby bird to her older sister
but the big girl said, "Yecccch!
Put it down!"
The smaller girl kept holding it out,
shielding it from sun
with her other hand
and the big girl shouted, "I told you,
get rid of it!"
—squirting water
from a plastic bottle
on her sister and the bird.
The face of the younger girl,
stunned in the courthouse square.
Pressed-in pair of wings.
Scared heart pounding.

The Word PEACE ～～～～～～～～～

We could find words or parts of words
inside other words, it was always a game.
PEACE for example contained the crucial vowels of
EAT and EASY. If people ATE together
they would be less likely to KILL one another
especially if one were responsible for
     shopping & cooking
& the other for serving & cleaning
     & you took turns.
Then you started thinking, *What does he like?*
What might suit his fancy?
There should of course be meals
at all peace talks,
as there is eating at festivals & birthdays,
the generous platter, the giant bowl.
Those who placed a minor faith in rhyme,
might try PEACE & CEASE, as in,
could you please CEASE this hideous
waste of time & resources, world?
Had some people forgotten
just how lucky we are

to be BORN? People had grown too far
from the source, that's for sure.
A man said ETHICS as if it were
a dirty word.
And what about apologizing to kids?
After TEACHing us to use words to solve
our differences, what did adults do?
People two years old were starting to look
a lot better than anyone else
& consider their vocabularies.
EAT was probably in there.
Sweet DREAMS & PLEASE which also contained
those crucial vowels found in PEACE
if anyone were still thinking about it.
This didn't always work though,
because some might say WAR contained
the first two letters of ART
& you would not want them
for one minute to believe that.

To the Tree Frogs
Outside the Window 〜〜〜〜〜

Tree frogs, we were born wrong.
Why didn't we get a song like you?
Something we could all sing together?
In the big dark, strumming our throats?
All night, branches alive outside our screens,
you paddle the long boat,
nothing could sink
on a note like yours.
I'd press myself against that twisty bark,
be part of the leaves.
I'd shrink, stretch free
of these heavy syllables,
curving perfectly into chorus,
something we could all sing
together, yes

Messages from Everywhere

light up our backyard.
A bird that flew five thousand miles
is trilling six bright notes.
This bird flew over mountains and valleys
and tiny dolls and pencils
of children I will never see.
Because this bird is singing to me,
I belong to the wide wind,
the people far away who share
the air and the clouds.
Together we are looking up
into all we do not own
and we are listening.

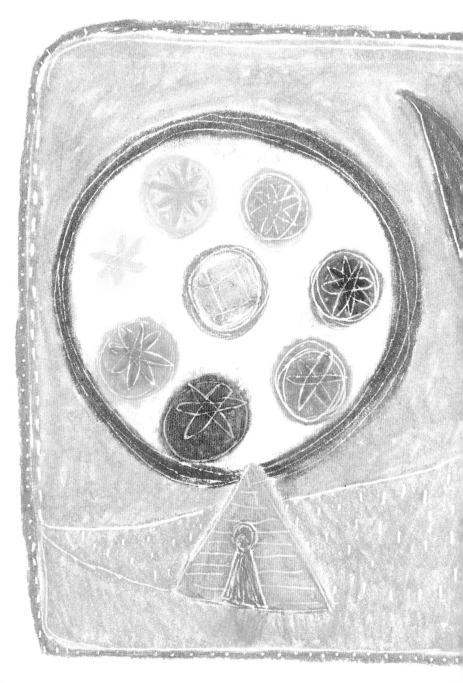

SECTION FIVE

Something True

Day After Halloween, Jack-o'-Lantern Candle All Burned Out

at dawn
on the sidewalk
a single shiny crow
pecking the stringy heart of a
pumpkin
exactly the same color as
sky

What Travel Does ~~~~~~~~~~~~

My uncle comes home from Siberia
describing the smoked caribou leg
still wearing its hoof
left on the drainboard
week after week,
small knives slicing
sour red flesh.
He becomes a vegetarian.
But he misses the spaciousness.
It wasn't crowded up there.
He ran into a polar bear
the same way you might run into your
mailman around the block.

My teacher returns from China
obsessed by the two-string violin
and the tiny birds in lattice cages.
She plays a tape
as we do our silent reading.

My whole family comes back from Paris
asking why we live anywhere else.
Every interesting person
and tucked neck scarf
looked full of stories.
People paused for peach tarts and crepes
in the middle of the afternoon.

My grandfather comes home
from Palestine
older.
He has been in the camps.
He can't stop aching.

After Mexico, my neighbor Lupe
misses intense color,
won't wear beige anymore.
She prefers papayas sliced
with lime juice drizzled on top.
She feels happy every time she faces south.

Abandoned Post Office, Big Bend

Forty years ago this postal window
far far far from any city
closed for good.
Where did everyone go?
Wooden cubbyholes
bear family names:
Wilson, Gibbs, Ramirez, Talley.

Someone has mailed them
dust.

Puff of wind
special delivery
and a little smoke rises.

Hello?

How much hope
how many thin slivers
long whistles
linen envelopes
found you here?
Did you ever go a year
without mail?

Beyond us every direction
desert   mountains   sky
write letters back and forth all day.
Tarantula scribbles a stone.
Fat-tailed fox signs with a flourish.

People aren't your kind anymore:
Wilson, Gibbs, Ramirez, Talley.
We're not that tough.

We have a car and bottles of water.
Each other's voices holding us up.

Learning to Talk

In some places
you can feel
perfect bird-lit air
with human talk nudged up against.
Talk and the velvet drapery of silence.
Deep evening echoes stitched by doves.

That's how I want to talk.
Not *chatter chatter chatter.*
Well, sometimes *chatter chatter chatter*
but also solid as adobe without cracks.
Also, *water in the well.*
Listen listen listen.

Hard to put together the pink hems
of sunrise and sunset
and the talkers on TV.
People beat talk into a froth.
Whip it up like a beverage.
We not only *say*
but say we're going to say
and say we said.

O kiss the silent ground!
The cool place under the bummiest cactus!

There was a cat with no tail
darted out from behind a yucca this morning
little gray sparrow snagged in his teeth
shamelessly doing what he was born to do
and NOT ONE WORD.

Over the Weather ~~~~~~~

We forget about the spaciousness above the clouds
but
it's up there.

The sun's up there too.

When words we hear don't fit the day,
when we worry
what we did or didn't do,
what if we close our eyes,
say any word we love
that makes us feel calm,
slip it into the atmosphere
and rise?

Creamy miles of quiet.
Giant swoop of blue.

On the Sunset Limited Train ~~

In the dining car, the couple from New Jersey
pressed their faces to the windows, anxious
for what they had waited all their lives to see,
the Pecos River and its high, brave bridge.

Good thing it is light, my dad said.
The sun had just risen.
When did you first start thinking about it?

So long ago! They stared at one another, shining.
West of the Pecos, such wonderful words!
Because that is the wild true land
beginning from there,
from the tall cliffs and the green river gash,
unfolding west, the land is stronger than anything,
it is the old song of land and air
we have never gotten to sing.

And we who had seen it many times
faced the glorious window
filled with the breaking light of day.

Across the Aisle

The little girl
with a floppy purple hair ribbon
coughed her way
across the Atlantic.
She coughed every 30 seconds
for seven whole hours.
No wonder she was fussy
before the plane took off,
pulling her father's pant leg,
and whining.
Something had gotten into her,
a whale trapped in her tiny lungs,
a restless pressing dolphin,

and she would be tied into a seat
for hours while it tried to get out.
She never once covered her mouth.
I felt angry at her father and mother
who seemed not to have discovered
cough syrup, cough drops,
or hot tea with lemon and honey.
38,000 feet below us
waves were roiling up
from a deep darkness in the sea
and fish who do not mind the cold
were gliding around in secrecy.

Mona's Taco ～～～～～～～～～～

Dear Mona, do you know
how your old stucco building
marks the spot of Something True?
Your hand-lettered red sign rises up
like a crooked, friendly flag.
I can guess the menu:
bean & cheese, potato & egg,
maybe a specialty of your own making,
avocado twist or smoky salsa.
Your *nombre* is nice.
One taco might be enough.
You feed the ranchers who just lived through
the worst drought and flood back-to-back.
They touch the brims of their hats
when they see you.
Don't we all need someone to greet us
to make us feel alive?

West of town, soft fields
ease our city-cluttered eyes.
There's a rim of hills to hope for up ahead.
Mona, mysterious Mona,
I don't have to eat with you to love you.
Every morning I think, *Mona's up.*

A Way Around

Argument
is a room I won't enter.
Some of us
would circle a whole house
not to enter it.

If you want to talk like that,
try a tree.
A tree is patient.
Don't try me.

To My Texas Handbook ~~~~~~~~~~~~~~

Don't ever say
there's nothing to see
in Ruidosa.

That's mean.

If you are really Texas
or Minnesota or North Dakota
or Georgia or Ohio
you should know
there's something strong to see
everywhere.

Over
and out.

Thoughts That Came in Floating

1

The land waits for rain to write on it.
Pool of birdseed, ring around the moon.
Night, that beautiful dark broom,
sweeps the day away.

2

But people are still fighting.
Far off, where we can't see or hear them.
We can barely imagine
our own familiar neighborhoods
blowing up—poof!
Everything being broken or gone.
So dumb!
No kid in the world wakes up hoping
people will fight around her house
or inside it either.

3

Electric networks
under the thin skin of hours,
ticking, stretching…

Two jackrabbits pause
in the long grasses of the orchard
side by side…

I want to talk truly as a rooster . . .

Hide inside a pocket of days . . .

4

My mind

is always

open.

I don't think

there's even

a door.

Index of first lines ~~~~~~~~~